By Definition

By Definition

POEMS OF FEELINGS

BY SARA HOLBROOK

Illustrations by Scott Mattern

WORDSONG

Boyds Mills Press

To Stephanie and Benjamin,
who in defining themselves
have redefined me

—S. H.

The poet wishes to thank Jane Yolen for her
generous spirit and editorial guidance.

The following poems have been previously published:

"Amused," "Evolution," "Investments," "Honesty," "Disappointment," "Lies," and "Jealous" in *Walking on the Boundaries of Change: Poems of Transition.* Copyright © 1998 by Sara Holbrook.

"Labels," "Subtle," and "Sorry" in *Am I Naturally This Crazy?* Copyright © 1996 by Sara Holbrook.

"Kind," "Doubt," "Angry," "Pout," and "Good Grief" in *I Never Said I Wasn't Difficult.* Copyright © 1996 by Sara Holbrook.

"Mistrust" in *The Dog Ate My Homework.* Copyright © 1996 by Sara Holbrook.

"Love" (previously titled "This Love and That") in *Which Way to the Dragon!: Poems for the Coming-on-Strong.* Copyright © 1996 by Sara Holbrook.

"My Dreams" in *Nothing's the End of the World.* Copyright © 1995 by Sara Holbrook.

"Alone" in *Wham! It's a Poetry Jam: Discovering Performance Poetry.* Copyright © 2002 by Sara Holbrook.

Published by Wordsong • Boyds Mills Press, Inc. • A Highlights Company
815 Church Street • Honesdale, Pennsylvania 18431
Printed in China

Publisher Cataloging-in-Publication Data (U.S.)

Holbrook, Sara.
By definition : poems of feelings / by Sara Holbrook ; illustrations by Scott Mattern.—1st ed.
[48] p. : ill. ; cm.
Includes index.
Summary: Poems for adolescents and teenagers that touch upon issues such as love, disappointment, honesty, and maturity.
ISBN 1-59078-060-4 hc • ISBN 1-59078-085-X pb
1. Emotions—Juvenile poetry. 2. Children's poetry, American.
(1. Emotions—Poetry. 2. American poetry.) I. Mattern, Scott. II. Title. 811.54 21 2003
2002108959

First edition, 2003
Book designed by Jeff George
The text of this book is set in 12-point New Century Schoolbook.

Visit our Web site at www.boydsmillspress.com

10 9 8 7 6 5 4 3 2 1 hc
10 9 8 7 6 5 4 3 2 1 pb

Contents

Introduction

An outward display—
    Words on paper,
aligned like birds on wires,
they sit a bit,
chat and chit,
flap and flit
       A W A Y !
Defining who we are
by what we choose to say.

In a world of action and reaction, it sometimes
seems as if words are an endangered species.
More than ever, we must with relentless defiance
continue to nurture our words, respect them as
individuals, and handle them with care.

Sara.

Procrastinator

A perpetual waiter,

      never just late,

always

    later.

Amused

A muse.
The accidental thought,
the sticky ruse
my daydreams brought
that always makes me
tardier than bells.
Till someone yells
and hurry pushes
my dawdle to respond,
but not for long.
Again! I'm
interrupted by temptation,
another brief examination
of the mossy side of memory
kicked over in a haste.
I stop for just a taste,
the world will have to wait.
Again.
Again.
I'm late.

Adrenaline

Made you run.
Made you run.

        Thanks a lot,
        adrenaline.

Stop your whining.
I got you there.

        Yeah—like a panting dog
        with stand-up hair.

You would have arrived
sometime next week.

        You blew my cool.
        You made me freak.

I like to push you
to the max.

        Great.
        Now take a hike,
        and I'll relax.

Evolution

TV came
out of radio,
free verse
came out of rhyme.
I am
coming out of middle school,
changing all the time.
It's time
to lose the water wings,
crawl out of this lagoon.
I want to stand upright.
Get on my feet.
I want it soon.

Paradox

Mowing the yard
is grass in the nose,
hugging the edge,
avoiding the hose,
dumping the clippings,
filling the tank.
A pain in my summer.

Cash in the bank.

Labels

People get tagged with these labels,
like African American,
Native American,
White,
Asian, Hispanic,
or Euro-Caucasian—
I just ask that you get my name right.
I'm part Willie,
part Ethel,
part Suzi and Scott.
Part assembly-line worker,
part barber, a lot of dancer
and salesman. Part grocer and mailman.
Part rural, part city, part cook,
and part caveman.
I'm a chunk-style vegetable soup
of cultural little bits,
my recipe's unique,
and no one label fits.
Grouping folks together
is an individual waste.
You can't know me by just a look,
you have to take a taste.

Curiosity

Curiosity's
a peeper
watching with shrewd eyes,
bold about the room
or keyhole-sneaking
shy.

It can't stand
keeping secrets,
it wants an answer NOW.
Can't trust
that things just work,
it has to know
just
how.

Curiosity's
insistence
asks ten million whys.
Proud of
its persistence,
it
exposes hidden lies.

Kind

Is it kind to be kind,
or am I a chump?
If I lend you a hand,
if I smile when you grump,
am I stupid?
A doormat?
A worm?
Or a fool?
Is it dumb to be kind?
Are selfish and cruel
always smart?
Weren't we born
with both brains
and a heart?

Happiness

Happiness comes hopping
when work is finished,
or
it brightens up my windows
and rattles at my door
with news that something's
coming.
Excitement's standing near.

Its hop-hop-happy hopping
jumps right over
doubt and fear.

And though
I know it's goofy,
if I watch it for a while,
that hop-hop-happy hopping
always makes me smile.

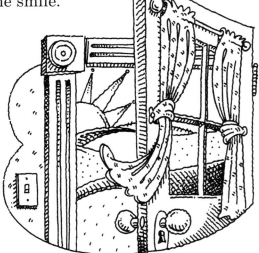

Investments

Securities
I've borrowed
from the pockets
of your mind
and tucked them
secret places
to be returned
in kind.
A valuable investment
in friendship
has been made,
accumulating interest
in trust
for future trade.

Basic Physics

You and me
and energy
compound when we are paired.
Add Mark and Ray
and a breath of May,
and E = us two squared.

When finally spring
starts happening,
we spark like fossil fuel
to explode against
all grown-up sense
and that bottleneck
called school.

Checkups

A friendship should
have checkups—
pressure,
weight,
temperature,
eyes and ears—
before it suffers from neglect,
overextends,
or breaks out
in a case
of terminal tears.

Whatever

So.
Which one is it?
Can't be
truth in both those two:
pretending you don't like me,
pretending that you do.

I'm putting on my coat.
Which of them's a lie?
If you just say,
"Whatever,"
then
I'll just say,
"Good-bye."

Honesty

Honesty
trying
is more than
just simply
the absence
of
lying.

Mistrust

What truth wraps up,
mistrust unties.

You can't hold
friends
in a
pack
of lies.

Subtle

Subtle
isn't a punch in the nose,
a kick in the shins,
a bee in the toes.

Subtle
stays quiet,
yet
everyone knows.

Disappointment

Disappointment!
What a surprise—
You're a blast from door's-open cold.
You're nuts in my chocolate cream.
You're a late lunch
        and bread sprouting mold.

Disappointment?
You're a blister from new favorite shoes.
You promised, and then you forgot.
You're just crumbs where there
        once was a cake.
You looked honest, but then you were not.

Disappointment:
You took pliers and yanked out my trust
like a dentist without Novocaine.
Then you didn't return my calls
when I tried to express my pain.

Doubt

Insecure
is a lace
untied
that in a race
trips me inside.

It hints
that I don't
have the stuff,
why try,
when I'm not good enough.
And once
I stumble
in my mind,
it's harder
not to fall behind.

It sure would be
a faster route
if I could live
without a doubt.

Stuck

Sometimes
Unhappy
has nowhere to go
but sit there in my chest.
It lacks plans
for tomorrow
so gets stuck
in nothingness.

Angry

You can't hold me,
      angry, angry.
When I'm angry,
      angry, angry.
There's no comfort
in your touching when I'm mad.

If you talk to me, I'll fight you.
If you reach for me, I'll bite you,
      'cause I'm angry,
      'cause I'm angry,
      'cause I'm mad.

Though at first it wasn't you,
I was mad, but not at you,
till you held me,
or you tried
to push my mad aside.

I'm a raging storm inside.
You can't hold me,
and you tried.
Now I'm angry 'cause you tried.

Now I'm angry with an anger
you can't hold and I can't hide.
      Angry, angry,
      angry, angry.
Can't control me,
      angry, angry.
You can't hold me,
      angry, angry.
So don't try.

Voice of Authority

Fiery-red neck,
marble-blue eyes
demand:
> *Can't you just prioritize?*

As if feelings,
heartaches,
self-made moods
have no purpose.
That attitudes
lack control.
In a finger snap
you say:
> *Get a hold*
> *and you'll be fine.*
> *Act adult.*
> *Change your mind.*

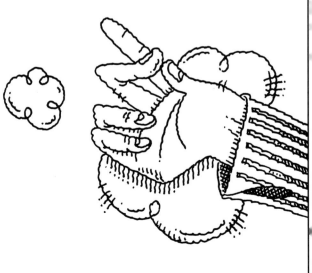

Pout

No use
acting nice to me
when I'm stuck
in a pout.
I can't let your
niceness in
until my mad
wears
out.

Nearly Distant

Families,
kitchen magnets,
repel each time
they turn their backs—
distancing themselves
when they should
listen,
not react.

Afterthoughts

Thoughts love.
They look.
Eye-brood
    or smile.
Thoughts blurt,
race-rush,
    or wait awhile.

Thoughts trapped inside
may blame
    and boil.
Review. React.
    Replay. Recoil.

Thoughts expressed
    may find a way
to take a stand,
    find solutions,
lend a hand.

Those thoughts
that can't find words
    exist,
      resist,
        insist
          unheard.

Sorry

Sorry
follows like my shadow,
fastened at the heels.
It trails me to my room
and sits with me at meals.

It nags me in my dreams
when I have gone to bed.
That Sorry pest hangs on
until
it's finally said.

Imagine

I imagine.
It merry-go-rounds
my mind,
wild-eyed
wooden horses dance
to life as music
winds around some fact.
Up and over and back.
Up and over and back.
Bound to that central fact,
one tiny, powerful gear,
locked tooth to tooth with fear,
driving horses, music, dancing
around,
around,
advancing how I feel.
Expanding what is real.
I imagine.

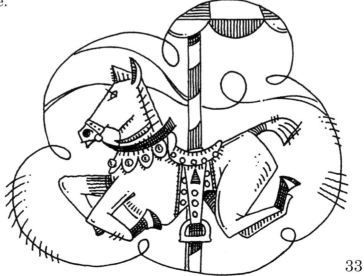

My Dreams

Open
window by my bed,
the EXIT
for my dreams.
Among the light-lured bugs,
mobbed against the screen,
my dreams
step out at night,
stretch,
and vanish
out of sight.

Reality

The future,
a real
blabbermouth
who always
has its say.
It interrupts
my fantasies
in passing
day-by-day.

Dreams
think they know
what will be.
But time acts
out reality.

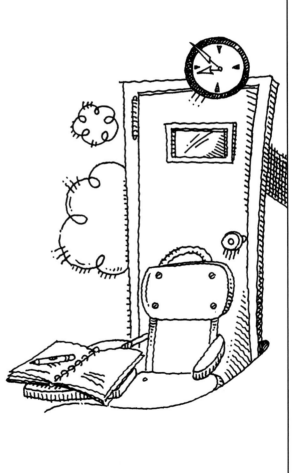

Trophies

I said it was too hard.
I almost ran and hid.
I didn't want to do it.
But don't you know—
I DID!

Accomplishment's
a chore,
wrestling with self,
victorious,
admired,
then placed on
a shelf.

That trophy is
my sigh of relief,
my pat on the back,
a reminder that
I can beat
myself
when I
stay on track.

Good Grief

Grief gets worn out by grieving.
Pain's a coat I must put on
and wear around the house
till it no longer feels so wrong.
I can't leave it in the box
and claim it doesn't fit.
I can't bag it for the coat drive
or wait
till I grow into it.
Not a color of my choosing,
and nothing to brag about.
The sooner
I try grief on,
the sooner grief
will get worn out.

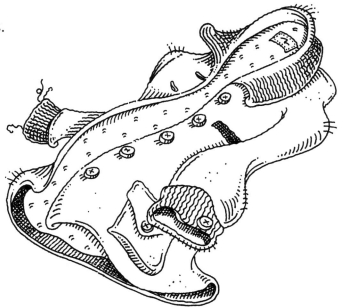

The Guest

Hope
is the guest
who's welcomed back,
can't overstay,
and won't unpack.

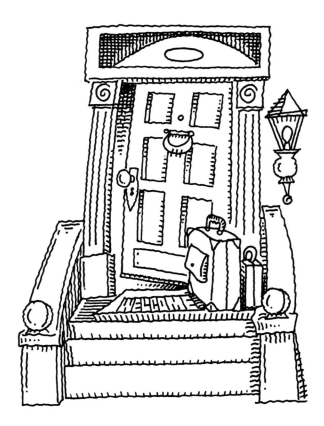

Analogy

Poetry is to verse
as love is to affection—
both a welcome comforter
on long December nights.
But only one
presumes
to warm
the heart.

Love

I've noticed there's a difference
between
this love
and that.
I really love my mother.
I really love my cat.

Some feelings are called
love,
though they don't feel the same.
I guess because like everything,
they have to have a
name.

Love acts in the movies.
Love talks on TV.
My favorite kind of love
feels warm
inside of me.
It hugs me
when I'm hopeless
and won't leave me
alone.
When I give
a piece away—
it always
comes back home.

Lies

I got burned, but
you can't say I'm abused.
I'm just down
and feeling used.
My eyes are dark
but dry,
no one knows
about the lie.

I never should have smiled
and said
that everything's all right.
I should have said,
"Hold on,"
but I was scared to spark a fight.

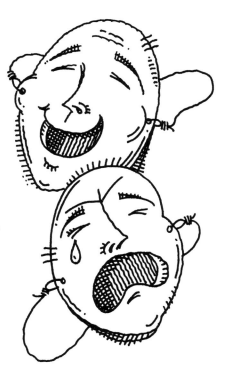

When I'm all buffed up
in smiles,
you can't say I'm victimized.
This arson is my crime.
I set fire to my insides
with a lie,
a smile
that let my hurting
hide.

Jealous

One-on-one,
Jealous
jump-reacts,
fouling out
when tossed a fact,
as sportsmanlike
as a shove out-of-bounds,
 a blind side that
 leaves you sprawling flat.
 An unfair, nose-to-the-ground,
 low-down put-down.
And just about as fun.

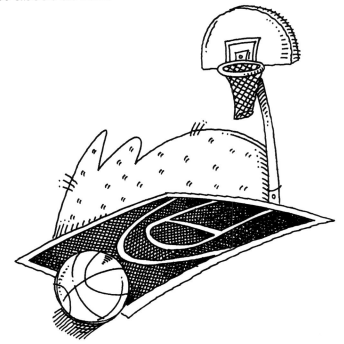

Pardon Me

My sorest pain
of any kind
was fixed with smiles
and
"Never mind."

Alone

Alone
doesn't have to be sad
like a lost-in-the-city dog.

Alone
doesn't have to be scary
like a vampire swirled in fog.

Alone
can be slices of quiet,
salami in between
a month of pushy hallways
and nights too tired to dream.

Alone
doesn't have to be
a scrimmage game with grief.
Alone
doesn't have to argue,
make excuses, or compete.
Like having nothing due,
sometimes,
Alone
is a relief.

Luck

Luck is the sun
on a warm July day,
but it won't pack the pickles
or chase ants away.

Today is my picnic.
I fill up the basket.
Luck
may come along,
but I won't wait to ask it.

Vacation

Vacation
takes me places
       where
I can't ever say
I've never been
          before
     again.

And when a place is
different, I am
       different, too.
I can look outside
and in
         and still enjoy
    the view.

Home is
only one place,
    here,
I'm always surrounded by same,
       expected to wear certain colors
    and always act like my name.

Vacation
takes me places,
     there
I shop for the unknown.
Try on something new.
       Pocket the change,
   and bring it home.

Uplift

Elation
appears
without foundation
and practical ties.
All-you-want
FREE BALLOONS!
Primary thoughts
that swell

        up, up

my insides.
Jump and reach!
We're on the rise—
yellow, red—against

        azure skies.

Index